Dieses Angelbuch gehört:

____

Datum: ____

Ort: ____

Geangelt habe ich heute mit: _______________________

Diesen Köder habe ich verwendet: ___________________

So war das Wetter heute: ___________________________

Mein Fang des Tages:

Mein Angelausflug war:

Meine Angelnotizen:

Fang des Tages

Datum: ____

Ort: ____

Geangelt habe ich heute mit: __________________________

Diesen Köder habe ich verwendet: ______________________

So war das Wetter heute: ______________________________

Mein Fang des Tages:

Mein Angelausflug war:

Meine Angelnotizen:

Fang des Tages

Datum: _______________________________________

Ort: ____

Geangelt habe ich heute mit: ___________________

Diesen Köder habe ich verwendet: ______________

So war das Wetter heute: ______________________

Mein Fang des Tages:

Mein Angelausflug war:

Meine Angelnotizen:

Fang des Tages

Datum: ____

Ort: ____

Geangelt habe ich heute mit: _________________________

Diesen Köder habe ich verwendet: _____________________

So war das Wetter heute: _____________________________

Mein Fang des Tages:

Mein Angelausflug war:

Meine Angelnotizen:

Fang des Tages

Datum: _______________________________________

Ort: ____

Geangelt habe ich heute mit: __________________

Diesen Köder habe ich verwendet: ______________

So war das Wetter heute: ______________________

Mein Fang des Tages:

Mein Angelausflug war:

Meine Angelnotizen:

Fang des Tages

Datum: ____

Ort: ____

Geangelt habe ich heute mit: _________________________

Diesen Köder habe ich verwendet: _____________________

So war das Wetter heute: _____________________________

Mein Fang des Tages:

Mein Angelausflug war:

Meine Angelnotizen:

Fang des Tages

Datum: _______________________________

Ort: _______________________________

Geangelt habe ich heute mit: _______________________________

Diesen Köder habe ich verwendet: _______________________________

So war das Wetter heute: _______________________________

Mein Fang des Tages:

Mein Angelausflug war:

Meine Angelnotizen:

Fang des Tages

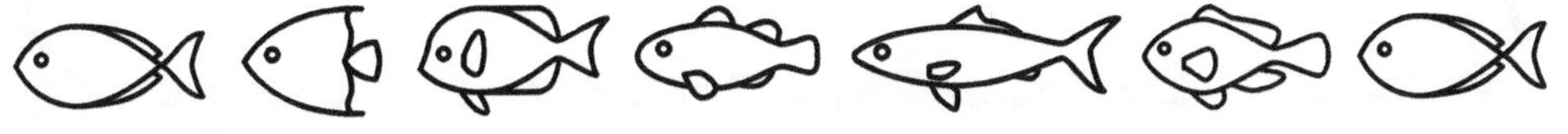

Datum: ____

Ort: ____

Geangelt habe ich heute mit: _____________________________

Diesen Köder habe ich verwendet: _________________________

So war das Wetter heute: ________________________________

Mein Fang des Tages:

Mein Angelausflug war:

Meine Angelnotizen:

Fang des Tages

Datum: _______________________________________

Ort: ____

Geangelt habe ich heute mit: ___________________

Diesen Köder habe ich verwendet: _______________

So war das Wetter heute: _______________________

Mein Fang des Tages:

Mein Angelausflug war:

Meine Angelnotizen:

Fang des Tages

Datum: _______________________________________

Ort: ____

Geangelt habe ich heute mit: _____________________

Diesen Köder habe ich verwendet: _________________

So war das Wetter heute: _________________________

Mein Fang des Tages:

Mein Angelausflug war:

Meine Angelnotizen:

Fang des Tages

Datum: ____

Ort: ____

Geangelt habe ich heute mit: ___________________________

Diesen Köder habe ich verwendet: _______________________

So war das Wetter heute: _______________________________

Mein Fang des Tages:

Mein Angelausflug war:

Meine Angelnotizen:

Fang des Tages

Datum: ____

Ort: ____

Geangelt habe ich heute mit: _____________________________

Diesen Köder habe ich verwendet: _________________________

So war das Wetter heute: _________________________________

Mein Fang des Tages:

Mein Angelausflug war:

Meine Angelnotizen:

Fang des Tages

Datum: _______________________________________

Ort: ____

Geangelt habe ich heute mit: ___________________

Diesen Köder habe ich verwendet: ______________

So war das Wetter heute: _______________________

Mein Fang des Tages:

Mein Angelausflug war:

Meine Angelnotizen:

Fang des Tages

Datum: _______________________________________

Ort: ____

Geangelt habe ich heute mit: _____________________

Diesen Köder habe ich verwendet: _________________

So war das Wetter heute: _________________________

Mein Fang des Tages:

Mein Angelausflug war:

Meine Angelnotizen:

Fang des Tages

Datum: ____

Ort: ____

Geangelt habe ich heute mit: ____________________________

Diesen Köder habe ich verwendet: ________________________

So war das Wetter heute: ________________________________

Mein Fang des Tages:

Mein Angelausflug war:

Meine Angelnotizen:

Fang des Tages

Datum: ______________________________

Ort: ______________________________

Geangelt habe ich heute mit: ______________________________

Diesen Köder habe ich verwendet: ______________________________

So war das Wetter heute: ______________________________

Mein Fang des Tages:

Mein Angelausflug war:

Meine Angelnotizen:

Fang des Tages

Datum: ____

Ort: ____

Geangelt habe ich heute mit: ___________________________

Diesen Köder habe ich verwendet: _______________________

So war das Wetter heute: _______________________________

Mein Fang des Tages:

Mein Angelausflug war:

Meine Angelnotizen:

Fang des Tages

Datum: ____

Ort: ____

Geangelt habe ich heute mit: ________________________

Diesen Köder habe ich verwendet: ____________________

So war das Wetter heute: ____________________________

Mein Fang des Tages:

Mein Angelausflug war:

Meine Angelnotizen:

Fang des Tages

Datum: _______________________________________

Ort: ____

Geangelt habe ich heute mit: ____________________

Diesen Köder habe ich verwendet: _______________

So war das Wetter heute: _______________________

Mein Fang des Tages:

Mein Angelausflug war:

Meine Angelnotizen:

Fang des Tages

Datum: ____

Ort: ____

Geangelt habe ich heute mit: ___________________

Diesen Köder habe ich verwendet: _______________

So war das Wetter heute: _______________________

Mein Fang des Tages:

Mein Angelausflug war:

Meine Angelnotizen:

Fang des Tages

Datum: _______________________________________

Ort: ____

Geangelt habe ich heute mit: __________________

Diesen Köder habe ich verwendet: ______________

So war das Wetter heute: ______________________

Mein Fang des Tages:

Mein Angelausflug war:

Meine Angelnotizen:

Fang des Tages

Datum: ___________________________________

Ort: _____________________________________

Geangelt habe ich heute mit: _______________

Diesen Köder habe ich verwendet: ___________

So war das Wetter heute: __________________

Mein Fang des Tages:

Mein Angelausflug war:

Meine Angelnotizen:

Fang des Tages

Datum: ____

Ort: ____

Geangelt habe ich heute mit: ____________________________

Diesen Köder habe ich verwendet: ________________________

So war das Wetter heute: ________________________________

Mein Fang des Tages:

Mein Angelausflug war:

Meine Angelnotizen:

Fang des Tages

Datum: _______________________________________

Ort: ____

Geangelt habe ich heute mit: ____________________

Diesen Köder habe ich verwendet: _______________

So war das Wetter heute: _______________________

Mein Fang des Tages:

Mein Angelausflug war:

Meine Angelnotizen:

Fang des Tages

Datum: _______________________________

Ort: _______________________________

Geangelt habe ich heute mit: _______________________________

Diesen Köder habe ich verwendet: _______________________________

So war das Wetter heute: _______________________________

Mein Fang des Tages:

Mein Angelausflug war:

Meine Angelnotizen:

Fang des Tages

Datum: ______________________________

Ort: ______________________________

Geangelt habe ich heute mit: ______________________________

Diesen Köder habe ich verwendet: ______________________________

So war das Wetter heute: ______________________________

Mein Fang des Tages:

Mein Angelausflug war:

Meine Angelnotizen:

Fang des Tages

Datum: _______________________________________

Ort: ____

Geangelt habe ich heute mit: ___________________

Diesen Köder habe ich verwendet: _______________

So war das Wetter heute: _______________________

Mein Fang des Tages:

Mein Angelausflug war:

Meine Angelnotizen:

Fang des Tages

Datum: ____

Ort: ____

Geangelt habe ich heute mit: _____________________________

Diesen Köder habe ich verwendet: _________________________

So war das Wetter heute: ________________________________

Mein Fang des Tages:

Mein Angelausflug war:

Meine Angelnotizen:

Fang des Tages

Datum: ____

Ort: ____

Geangelt habe ich heute mit: ____________________________

Diesen Köder habe ich verwendet: _______________________

So war das Wetter heute: _______________________________

Mein Fang des Tages:

Mein Angelausflug war:

Meine Angelnotizen:

Fang des Tages

Datum: _______________________________________

Ort: ____

Geangelt habe ich heute mit: ____________________

Diesen Köder habe ich verwendet: ________________

So war das Wetter heute: _______________________

Mein Fang des Tages:

Mein Angelausflug war:

Meine Angelnotizen:

Fang des Tages

Datum: _______________________________________

Ort: ____

Geangelt habe ich heute mit: _________________

Diesen Köder habe ich verwendet: _____________

So war das Wetter heute: _____________________

Mein Fang des Tages:

Mein Angelausflug war:

Meine Angelnotizen:

Fang des Tages

Datum: _______________________________________

Ort: ____

Geangelt habe ich heute mit: ___________________

Diesen Köder habe ich verwendet: _______________

So war das Wetter heute: _______________________

Mein Fang des Tages:

Mein Angelausflug war:

Meine Angelnotizen:

Fang des Tages

Datum: _______________________________________

Ort: ____

Geangelt habe ich heute mit: __________________

Diesen Köder habe ich verwendet: ______________

So war das Wetter heute: ______________________

Mein Fang des Tages:

Mein Angelausflug war:

Meine Angelnotizen:

Fang des Tages

Datum: _______________________________

Ort: _______________________________

Geangelt habe ich heute mit: _______________________________

Diesen Köder habe ich verwendet: _______________________________

So war das Wetter heute: _______________________________

Mein Fang des Tages:

Mein Angelausflug war:

Meine Angelnotizen:

Fang des Tages

Datum: ____

Ort: ____

Geangelt habe ich heute mit: _________________________

Diesen Köder habe ich verwendet: _____________________

So war das Wetter heute: _____________________________

Mein Fang des Tages:

Mein Angelausflug war:

Meine Angelnotizen:

Fang des Tages

Datum: ______________________________________

Ort: ____

Geangelt habe ich heute mit: ________________________

Diesen Köder habe ich verwendet: ____________________

So war das Wetter heute: ____________________________

Mein Fang des Tages:

Mein Angelausflug war:

Meine Angelnotizen:

Fang des Tages

Datum: ____

Ort: ____

Geangelt habe ich heute mit: _________________________

Diesen Köder habe ich verwendet: _____________________

So war das Wetter heute: _____________________________

Mein Fang des Tages:

Mein Angelausflug war:

Meine Angelnotizen:

Fang des Tages

Datum: ____

Ort: ____

Geangelt habe ich heute mit: ____________________________

Diesen Köder habe ich verwendet: ________________________

So war das Wetter heute: ________________________________

Mein Fang des Tages:

Mein Angelausflug war:

Meine Angelnotizen:

Fang des Tages

Datum: _______________________________________

Ort: ____

Geangelt habe ich heute mit: _____________________

Diesen Köder habe ich verwendet: ________________

So war das Wetter heute: ________________________

Mein Fang des Tages:

Mein Angelausflug war:

Meine Angelnotizen:

Fang des Tages

Datum: _______________________________________

Ort: ____

Geangelt habe ich heute mit: _________________

Diesen Köder habe ich verwendet: _____________

So war das Wetter heute: _____________________

Mein Fang des Tages:

Mein Angelausflug war:

Meine Angelnotizen:

Fang des Tages

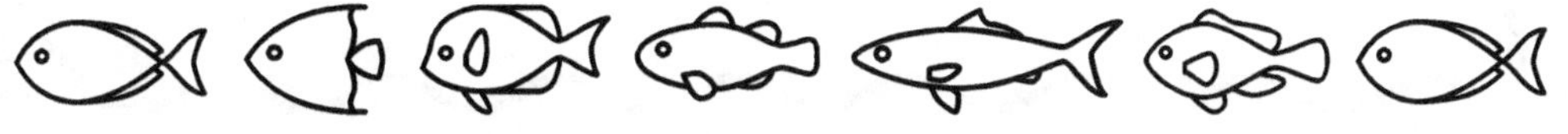

Datum: ___________________________________

Ort: _____________________________________

Geangelt habe ich heute mit: ______________

Diesen Köder habe ich verwendet: __________

So war das Wetter heute: __________________

Mein Fang des Tages:

Mein Angelausflug war:

Meine Angelnotizen:

Fang des Tages

Datum: ____

Ort: ____

Geangelt habe ich heute mit: _____________________________

Diesen Köder habe ich verwendet: _________________________

So war das Wetter heute: ________________________________

Mein Fang des Tages:

Mein Angelausflug war:

Meine Angelnotizen:

Fang des Tages

Datum: _______________________________________

Ort: ____

Geangelt habe ich heute mit: _____________________

Diesen Köder habe ich verwendet: _________________

So war das Wetter heute: _________________________

Mein Fang des Tages:

Mein Angelausflug war:

Meine Angelnotizen:

Fang des Tages

Datum: _______________________________

Ort: _________________________________

Geangelt habe ich heute mit: _______________

Diesen Köder habe ich verwendet: ______________

So war das Wetter heute: __________________

Mein Fang des Tages:

Mein Angelausflug war:

Meine Angelnotizen:

Fang des Tages

Datum: _______________________________________

Ort: ____

Geangelt habe ich heute mit: _____________________

Diesen Köder habe ich verwendet: _________________

So war das Wetter heute: _________________________

Mein Fang des Tages:

Mein Angelausflug war:

Meine Angelnotizen:

Fang des Tages

Datum: _______________________________________

Ort: ____

Geangelt habe ich heute mit: ___________________

Diesen Köder habe ich verwendet: _______________

So war das Wetter heute: _______________________

Mein Fang des Tages:

Mein Angelausflug war:

Meine Angelnotizen:

Fang des Tages

Datum: ____

Ort: ____

Geangelt habe ich heute mit: ____________________________

Diesen Köder habe ich verwendet: _______________________

So war das Wetter heute: _______________________________

Mein Fang des Tages:

Mein Angelausflug war:

Meine Angelnotizen:

Fang des Tages

Datum: ____

Ort: ____

Geangelt habe ich heute mit: __________________________

Diesen Köder habe ich verwendet: ______________________

So war das Wetter heute: ______________________________

Mein Fang des Tages:

Mein Angelausflug war:

Meine Angelnotizen:

Fang des Tages

Datum: _______________________________________

Ort: ____

Geangelt habe ich heute mit: __________________

Diesen Köder habe ich verwendet: _____________

So war das Wetter heute: ______________________

Mein Fang des Tages:

Mein Angelausflug war:

Meine Angelnotizen:

Fang des Tages

Datum: _______________________________________

Ort: ____

Geangelt habe ich heute mit: ___________________

Diesen Köder habe ich verwendet: _______________

So war das Wetter heute: _______________________

Mein Fang des Tages:

Mein Angelausflug war:

Meine Angelnotizen:

Fang des Tages

Datum: ____

Ort: ____

Geangelt habe ich heute mit: __________________________

Diesen Köder habe ich verwendet: ______________________

So war das Wetter heute: ______________________________

Mein Fang des Tages:

Mein Angelausflug war:

Meine Angelnotizen:

Fang des Tages

Datum: ______________________________

Ort: ______________________________

Geangelt habe ich heute mit: ______________________________

Diesen Köder habe ich verwendet: ______________________________

So war das Wetter heute: ______________________________

Mein Fang des Tages:

Mein Angelausflug war:

Meine Angelnotizen:

Fang des Tages

Datum: _______________________________________

Ort: ____

Geangelt habe ich heute mit: _____________________

Diesen Köder habe ich verwendet: _________________

So war das Wetter heute: ________________________

Mein Fang des Tages:

Mein Angelausflug war:

Meine Angelnotizen:

Fang des Tages

Datum: _______________________________________

Ort: ____

Geangelt habe ich heute mit: ___________________

Diesen Köder habe ich verwendet: ______________

So war das Wetter heute: ______________________

Mein Fang des Tages:

Mein Angelausflug war:

Meine Angelnotizen:

Fang des Tages

Datum: _______________________________________

Ort: ____

Geangelt habe ich heute mit: ____________________

Diesen Köder habe ich verwendet: _________________

So war das Wetter heute: _______________________

Mein Fang des Tages:

Mein Angelausflug war:

Meine Angelnotizen:

Fang des Tages

Datum: ____

Ort: ____

Geangelt habe ich heute mit: ____________________________

Diesen Köder habe ich verwendet: ________________________

So war das Wetter heute: _______________________________

Mein Fang des Tages:

Mein Angelausflug war:

Meine Angelnotizen:

Fang des Tages

Datum: _______________________________________

Ort: ____

Geangelt habe ich heute mit: ___________________

Diesen Köder habe ich verwendet: _______________

So war das Wetter heute: _______________________

Mein Fang des Tages:

Mein Angelausflug war:

Meine Angelnotizen:

Fang des Tages

Datum: _______________________________

Ort: _________________________________

Geangelt habe ich heute mit: _______________

Diesen Köder habe ich verwendet: ___________

So war das Wetter heute: __________________

Mein Fang des Tages:

Mein Angelausflug war:

Meine Angelnotizen:

Fang des Tages

Datum: _______________________________

Ort: _________________________________

Geangelt habe ich heute mit: ___________

Diesen Köder habe ich verwendet: _______

So war das Wetter heute: _______________

Mein Fang des Tages:

Mein Angelausflug war:

Meine Angelnotizen:

Fang des Tages

Datum: _______________________________

Ort: _________________________________

Geangelt habe ich heute mit: ___________

Diesen Köder habe ich verwendet: _______

So war das Wetter heute: _______________

Mein Fang des Tages:

Mein Angelausflug war:

Meine Angelnotizen:

www.ingramcontent.com/pod-product-compliance
Lightning Source LLC
Chambersburg PA
CBHW061738050726
47598CB00002B/539